50 Caribbean Cuisine Recipes for Home

By: Kelly Johnson

Table of Contents

- Jerk Chicken
- Coconut Rice and Peas
- Roti
- Ackee and Saltfish
- Callaloo Soup
- Curry Goat
- Trinidadian Doubles
- Rasta Pasta
- Conch Fritters
- Escovitch Fish
- Mango Salsa
- Caribbean Rum Punch
- Bajan Flying Fish Cutter
- Plantain Chips
- Johnny Cakes
- Pepper Pot Soup
- Grilled Snapper
- Caribbean Coleslaw
- Guava BBQ Ribs
- Sorrel Drink
- Stewed Oxtail
- Sweet Potato Pudding
- Pigeon Peas and Rice
- Bammy (Cassava Flatbread)
- Black Cake
- Curry Shrimp
- Jamaican Patty
- Cucumber Chutney
- Green Fig and Saltfish
- Barbados Cou-Cou
- Pineapple Ginger Chicken
- Creole Fish
- Goat Water Stew
- Tamarind Balls
- Soursop Smoothie

- Fried Dumplings
- Trinidadian Pelau
- Avocado Mango Salad
- Sea Moss Drink
- Coconut Bread
- Crab and Callaloo Dumplings
- Souse
- Peppered Shrimp
- Banana Fritters
- Fish Escabeche
- Pumpkin Soup
- Aloo Pie
- Grilled Lobster
- Pineapple Upside-Down Cake
- Seafood Roti

Jerk Chicken

Ingredients:

- 4 lbs chicken pieces (thighs, drumsticks, or a whole chicken cut into parts)
- 1/4 cup soy sauce
- 1/4 cup olive oil
- 3 tablespoons brown sugar
- 2 tablespoons ground allspice
- 1 tablespoon dried thyme
- 4 cloves garlic, minced
- 2 teaspoons ginger, grated
- 2-3 Scotch bonnet peppers, seeds removed and finely chopped (adjust to taste)
- 4 green onions, chopped
- 1 teaspoon black pepper
- 1 teaspoon cinnamon
- 1 teaspoon nutmeg
- Salt to taste

Instructions:

In a blender or food processor, combine soy sauce, olive oil, brown sugar, allspice, thyme, garlic, ginger, Scotch bonnet peppers, green onions, black pepper, cinnamon, and nutmeg. Blend until it forms a smooth paste.

Place the chicken pieces in a large bowl or resealable plastic bag. Rub the jerk seasoning all over the chicken, making sure it's well coated. For more intense flavor, you can let it marinate in the refrigerator for at least 4 hours, or preferably overnight.

Preheat your grill or oven to medium-high heat.

Grill the chicken for about 25-30 minutes, turning occasionally, until it's cooked through and has a nice char on the outside. If using an oven, you can bake the chicken at 375°F (190°C) for approximately 45-50 minutes.

Serve the Jerk Chicken with traditional sides like rice and peas, fried plantains, or coleslaw. Enjoy the bold and spicy flavors of this Caribbean favorite!

Coconut Rice and Peas

Ingredients:

- 2 cups long-grain rice
- 1 can (13.5 oz) coconut milk
- 1 cup water
- 1 cup canned kidney beans, drained and rinsed
- 1 small onion, finely chopped
- 2 cloves garlic, minced
- 1 sprig thyme
- 1 scallion, sliced
- 1 Scotch bonnet pepper (whole or sliced, depending on desired heat)
- 1 teaspoon salt
- 1/2 teaspoon black pepper
- 1 tablespoon vegetable oil

Instructions:

Rinse the rice under cold water until the water runs clear. This helps remove excess starch.

In a large pot or Dutch oven, heat the vegetable oil over medium heat. Add the chopped onion, minced garlic, and sliced scallion. Sauté for 2-3 minutes until the onions are translucent.

Pour in the coconut milk and water, then add the kidney beans, thyme, Scotch bonnet pepper, salt, and black pepper. Stir to combine.

Bring the mixture to a boil, then add the rinsed rice. Give it a good stir to ensure the rice is evenly distributed in the pot.

Reduce the heat to low, cover the pot, and simmer for 18-20 minutes or until the rice is tender and has absorbed the liquid. Avoid stirring the rice during this time to prevent it from becoming sticky.

Once the rice is cooked, fluff it with a fork to separate the grains. Remove the Scotch bonnet pepper and thyme sprig.

Serve the Coconut Rice and Peas hot as a delightful side dish to complement various Caribbean mains. Enjoy the rich coconut flavor and the subtle heat from the Scotch bonnet pepper!

Roti

Ingredients:

For the Roti Dough:

- 3 cups all-purpose flour
- 1 teaspoon baking powder
- 1 teaspoon salt
- 1 cup warm water

For Cooking:

- Vegetable oil or ghee (clarified butter)

Instructions:

In a large mixing bowl, combine the all-purpose flour, baking powder, and salt. Gradually add warm water to the flour mixture, stirring as you go, until a soft dough forms. Adjust the water if necessary to achieve a smooth consistency. Knead the dough on a floured surface for about 5-7 minutes until it becomes elastic and smooth.
Divide the dough into golf ball-sized portions.
Roll each ball into a smooth, round disc about 6-8 inches in diameter. Use a rolling pin and additional flour to prevent sticking.
Heat a griddle or non-stick skillet over medium-high heat.
Place a rolled-out roti onto the hot griddle and cook for about 1-2 minutes until bubbles start forming on the surface.
Flip the roti and cook the other side for an additional 1-2 minutes until both sides have a golden brown color.
While cooking, lightly brush each side of the roti with vegetable oil or ghee to enhance flavor and prevent sticking.
Repeat the process for the remaining dough balls.
Stack the cooked roti and keep them warm by wrapping them in a clean kitchen towel or aluminum foil.
Serve the roti with your favorite Caribbean dishes, such as curry, stew, or vegetables. Enjoy the soft and delicious texture of Caribbean roti!

Ackee and Saltfish

Ingredients:

- 1 pound salted codfish
- 1 can (19 oz) ackee, drained and rinsed
- 2 tablespoons vegetable oil
- 1 onion, finely chopped
- 1 bell pepper, diced (traditionally green, but any color works)
- 2 tomatoes, chopped
- 2 cloves garlic, minced
- 1 sprig thyme
- 2 green onions, sliced
- 1 Scotch bonnet pepper, seeds removed and finely chopped (adjust to taste)
- Salt and black pepper to taste

Instructions:

Start by preparing the salted codfish. Rinse the salted cod under cold running water to remove excess salt. Boil the codfish in water for about 15-20 minutes to further reduce saltiness. Drain and flake the codfish into small pieces.
Heat vegetable oil in a large skillet or frying pan over medium heat.
Add chopped onions, bell pepper, and garlic to the skillet. Sauté until the vegetables are softened and the onions are translucent.
Add the flaked codfish to the skillet, stirring well to combine with the vegetables.
Add chopped tomatoes, thyme, green onions, and Scotch bonnet pepper to the skillet. Cook for an additional 5-7 minutes, allowing the flavors to meld.
Gently fold in the drained ackee, being careful not to break the ackee into small pieces. Cook for an additional 3-5 minutes until the ackee is heated through.
Season the dish with salt and black pepper to taste. Be cautious with the salt, as the codfish may still have some residual saltiness.
Remove the sprig of thyme and serve the Ackee and Saltfish hot. It's commonly paired with fried plantains, breadfruit, or dumplings.

Enjoy this delicious and iconic Jamaican dish!

Callaloo Soup

Ingredients:

- 1 bunch callaloo (or substitute with spinach), washed and chopped
- 1 cup okra, sliced
- 1 cup pumpkin, diced
- 1 medium onion, chopped
- 2 cloves garlic, minced
- 1 medium carrot, diced
- 1 medium potato, diced
- 1 can (15 oz) red kidney beans, drained and rinsed
- 1 can (14 oz) coconut milk
- 6 cups vegetable or chicken broth
- 2 tablespoons vegetable oil
- 1 teaspoon thyme, dried or fresh
- 1 Scotch bonnet pepper, whole (optional, for heat)
- Salt and black pepper to taste

Instructions:

In a large pot, heat the vegetable oil over medium heat. Add chopped onions and minced garlic, sautéing until the onions are translucent.

Add diced pumpkin, carrot, and potato to the pot. Stir and cook for about 5 minutes.

Pour in the vegetable or chicken broth, and add the thyme and Scotch bonnet pepper (if using). Bring the mixture to a boil, then reduce the heat to simmer.

Add sliced okra to the pot and continue simmering for another 10-15 minutes until the vegetables are tender.

Stir in the chopped callaloo (or spinach) and cook for an additional 3-5 minutes until the greens are wilted.

Pour in the coconut milk and add the drained red kidney beans. Stir well and let the soup simmer for another 5-7 minutes.

Season the soup with salt and black pepper to taste. Adjust the heat level by removing the Scotch bonnet pepper if it's reached your desired spice level.

Remove the Scotch bonnet pepper and serve the Callaloo Soup hot. You can enjoy it as is or with a side of rice or bread.

This hearty and flavorful soup showcases the vibrant and diverse flavors of Caribbean cuisine.

Curry Goat

Ingredients:

- 2.5 to 3 pounds goat meat, cut into chunks
- 3 tablespoons curry powder
- 1 teaspoon allspice
- 1 teaspoon ground turmeric
- 1 teaspoon ground coriander
- 1 teaspoon cumin
- 1 large onion, chopped
- 4 cloves garlic, minced
- 2 inches ginger, grated
- 2 sprigs thyme
- 2-3 Scotch bonnet peppers, seeds removed and finely chopped (adjust to taste)
- 2 tablespoons vegetable oil
- 2 cups coconut milk
- 3 cups water or beef/chicken broth
- 2 large potatoes, peeled and diced
- Salt and black pepper to taste

Instructions:

In a bowl, combine the goat meat with curry powder, allspice, turmeric, coriander, and cumin. Massage the spices into the meat and let it marinate for at least 30 minutes, or preferably overnight in the refrigerator.

In a large, heavy-bottomed pot or Dutch oven, heat vegetable oil over medium heat.

Add chopped onions, minced garlic, grated ginger, thyme, and Scotch bonnet peppers. Sauté until the onions are translucent and the mixture is aromatic.

Add the marinated goat meat to the pot and brown it on all sides.

Pour in the coconut milk and water (or broth) to the pot, ensuring the meat is covered. Bring the mixture to a boil.

Reduce the heat to low, cover the pot, and simmer for 1.5 to 2 hours or until the goat meat is tender. Stir occasionally and add more water or broth if needed.

About 30 minutes before the meat is done, add diced potatoes to the pot.

Season the curry with salt and black pepper to taste.

Once the meat is tender and the potatoes are cooked, adjust the seasoning if necessary, and remove the thyme sprigs.
Serve the Curry Goat hot over rice or with traditional Caribbean side dishes like rice and peas, roti, or bread.

Enjoy this flavorful and hearty Caribbean curry dish!

Trinidadian Doubles

Ingredients:

For the Bara (Flatbread):

- 2 cups all-purpose flour
- 1 teaspoon baking powder
- 1/2 teaspoon ground turmeric
- 1/2 teaspoon ground cumin
- 1/2 teaspoon ground curry powder
- 1/2 teaspoon salt
- Water (approximately 1 to 1.5 cups) for making a soft dough
- Vegetable oil for frying

For the Channa (Chickpea Filling):

- 2 cans (15 oz each) chickpeas, drained and rinsed
- 1 large onion, finely chopped
- 3 cloves garlic, minced
- 1 teaspoon ground cumin
- 1 teaspoon ground coriander
- 1 teaspoon ground turmeric
- 1 teaspoon ground roasted geera (ground roasted cumin seeds)
- 1 teaspoon curry powder
- 1 teaspoon mustard (optional)
- 1 tablespoon vegetable oil
- Salt and pepper to taste
- Hot sauce (optional, for added heat)

Instructions:

For the Bara:

In a large mixing bowl, combine flour, baking powder, turmeric, cumin, curry powder, and salt.

Gradually add water to the dry ingredients, stirring to form a soft dough. Knead the dough for a few minutes until smooth.

Cover the dough and let it rest for about 30 minutes.

Divide the dough into golf ball-sized portions and roll each portion into a ball.

On a floured surface, roll each ball into a thin, flat disc (about 6 inches in diameter).

Heat vegetable oil in a frying pan over medium heat.

Fry the bara until golden brown on both sides. Drain on paper towels to remove excess oil.

For the Channa:

In a pan, heat vegetable oil over medium heat. Add chopped onions and sauté until translucent.

Add minced garlic and sauté for another minute.

Add ground cumin, coriander, turmeric, roasted geera, curry powder, and mustard (if using). Stir well to coat the onions and garlic with the spices.

Add chickpeas to the pan and stir to combine. Cook for 5-7 minutes.

Season with salt and pepper to taste. If desired, add hot sauce for extra heat.

Assembling the Doubles:

Place a spoonful of the channa mixture onto one bara.

Top with another bara, creating a sandwich.

Repeat with the remaining bara and channa.

Serve Trinidadian Doubles hot and enjoy this delicious street food!

Trinidadian Doubles are often served with various chutneys and sauces for added flavor.

Rasta Pasta

Ingredients:

- 8 oz (about 225g) penne or your favorite pasta
- 1 lb (about 450g) chicken breasts, thinly sliced
- 2 tablespoons jerk seasoning (store-bought or homemade)
- 1 tablespoon vegetable oil
- 1 onion, thinly sliced
- 1 bell pepper (any color), thinly sliced
- 1 cup cherry tomatoes, halved
- 3 cloves garlic, minced
- 1 can (14 oz) coconut milk
- 2 tablespoons tomato paste
- 1 teaspoon dried thyme
- 1 teaspoon paprika
- Salt and black pepper to taste
- Fresh parsley or cilantro for garnish
- Grated Parmesan cheese (optional)

Instructions:

Cook the pasta according to the package instructions until al dente. Drain and set aside.
In a bowl, coat the sliced chicken breasts with jerk seasoning. Ensure that the chicken is well coated, and let it marinate for at least 15-30 minutes.
In a large skillet or pan, heat vegetable oil over medium-high heat. Add the marinated chicken and cook until browned and cooked through. Remove the chicken from the pan and set it aside.
In the same pan, add a bit more oil if needed and sauté the sliced onion until softened.
Add the sliced bell pepper, cherry tomatoes, and minced garlic to the pan. Cook for a few minutes until the vegetables are slightly tender.
Pour in the coconut milk and add the tomato paste, dried thyme, and paprika. Stir well to combine.
Bring the mixture to a simmer and let it cook for about 5-7 minutes to allow the flavors to meld. Season with salt and black pepper to taste.

Add the cooked chicken back to the pan, stirring to coat it in the creamy sauce. Cook for an additional 2-3 minutes.

Toss the cooked pasta into the pan, ensuring it's well coated with the flavorful sauce.

Garnish the Rasta Pasta with fresh parsley or cilantro, and if desired, sprinkle with grated Parmesan cheese.

Serve hot and enjoy this vibrant and delicious Caribbean-inspired pasta dish!

Rasta Pasta is known for its fusion of flavors and colors, making it a delightful and satisfying meal.

Conch Fritters

Ingredients:

- 1 pound conch meat, finely chopped
- 1 cup all-purpose flour
- 1 teaspoon baking powder
- 1/2 teaspoon salt
- 1/4 teaspoon black pepper
- 1/4 teaspoon cayenne pepper (adjust to taste)
- 1/2 cup bell peppers, finely chopped (mix of red and green for color)
- 1/2 cup onion, finely chopped
- 1/4 cup celery, finely chopped
- 2 cloves garlic, minced
- 2 tablespoons fresh parsley, chopped
- 1 large egg, beaten
- 1/2 cup milk
- Vegetable oil for deep-frying
- Lemon wedges for serving
- Cocktail or tartar sauce for dipping

Instructions:

In a large mixing bowl, combine the all-purpose flour, baking powder, salt, black pepper, and cayenne pepper.

Add the finely chopped conch meat, bell peppers, onion, celery, garlic, and parsley to the dry ingredients. Mix well to combine.

In a separate bowl, whisk together the beaten egg and milk.

Pour the wet ingredients into the conch mixture and stir until everything is well combined. The batter should have a thick, but still pourable, consistency.

In a deep fryer or large, deep skillet, heat vegetable oil to 350°F (175°C).

Using a spoon or an ice cream scoop, drop portions of the batter into the hot oil, making sure not to overcrowd the pan.

Fry the conch fritters for about 3-4 minutes, turning them occasionally, until they are golden brown and crispy.

Use a slotted spoon to remove the fritters from the oil and place them on a paper towel-lined plate to absorb any excess oil.

Repeat the frying process with the remaining batter.

Serve the conch fritters hot with lemon wedges and your favorite dipping sauce, such as cocktail or tartar sauce.

Enjoy these crispy and flavorful conch fritters as a delicious appetizer or snack with a taste of the Caribbean!

Escovitch Fish

Ingredients:

For the Fried Fish:

- 2 pounds whole fish (snapper or any white fish), cleaned and scaled
- 1 cup all-purpose flour
- 1 teaspoon salt
- 1/2 teaspoon black pepper
- 1/2 teaspoon garlic powder
- Vegetable oil for frying

For the Pickled Vegetables (Escovitch Sauce):

- 1 cup thinly sliced carrots
- 1 cup thinly sliced bell peppers (assorted colors)
- 1 cup thinly sliced onions
- 2 Scotch bonnet peppers, thinly sliced (adjust to taste)
- 1 cup white vinegar
- 1/2 cup water
- 2 tablespoons sugar
- 1 teaspoon salt
- 6-8 pimento seeds (allspice berries)
- 4 sprigs thyme
- 4 tablespoons vegetable oil

Instructions:

Fried Fish:

Rinse and pat dry the whole fish.
In a bowl, mix together the flour, salt, black pepper, and garlic powder.
Dredge each fish in the seasoned flour mixture, ensuring they are well coated.
In a large skillet or frying pan, heat vegetable oil over medium-high heat.
Fry the fish for about 5-7 minutes on each side or until golden brown and cooked through. The cooking time will depend on the size and thickness of the fish.

Once fried, transfer the fish to a paper towel-lined plate to drain excess oil.

Pickled Vegetables (Escovitch Sauce):

In a saucepan, combine white vinegar, water, sugar, salt, pimento seeds, and thyme. Bring the mixture to a boil and let it simmer for 2-3 minutes.
In a separate skillet, heat vegetable oil over medium heat. Add sliced carrots, bell peppers, onions, and Scotch bonnet peppers. Sauté for 2-3 minutes until slightly softened but still crisp.
Pour the hot vinegar mixture over the sautéed vegetables. Stir to combine, ensuring the vegetables are well coated in the pickling liquid.
Allow the escovitch sauce to cool slightly.

Assembling:

Place the fried fish on a serving platter.
Spoon the pickled vegetables and the escovitch sauce over the top of the fried fish.
Garnish with additional thyme sprigs if desired.
Serve the Escovitch Fish with your favorite side dishes, such as rice and peas or fried plantains.

Enjoy this flavorful and tangy Jamaican dish that combines the crispy texture of fried fish with the zesty kick of pickled vegetables!

Mango Salsa

Ingredients:

- 2 ripe mangoes, peeled, pitted, and diced
- 1/2 red onion, finely chopped
- 1 red bell pepper, diced
- 1 jalapeño pepper, seeds removed and finely chopped
- 1/4 cup fresh cilantro, chopped
- Juice of 1 lime
- Salt and black pepper to taste

Instructions:

In a bowl, combine the diced mangoes, chopped red onion, diced red bell pepper, chopped jalapeño pepper, and chopped cilantro.
Squeeze the juice of one lime over the ingredients. Adjust the amount of lime juice according to your taste preferences.
Gently toss the ingredients together until well combined.
Season the mango salsa with salt and black pepper to taste. Start with a small amount and adjust according to your liking.
Let the salsa sit in the refrigerator for at least 30 minutes to allow the flavors to meld.
Before serving, give the salsa a final gentle toss.
Serve Mango Salsa as a topping for grilled chicken, fish, shrimp, or as a side dish with tacos and nachos.

Enjoy this vibrant and sweet Mango Salsa that adds a tropical twist to your favorite dishes!

Caribbean Rum Punch

Ingredients:

- 1 cup dark rum
- 1/2 cup light rum
- 1 cup pineapple juice
- 1 cup orange juice
- 1/4 cup grenadine syrup
- 3 tablespoons fresh lime juice
- 1 teaspoon Angostura bitters
- Pineapple slices, orange slices, and maraschino cherries for garnish
- Ice cubes

Instructions:

In a large pitcher, combine the dark rum, light rum, pineapple juice, orange juice, grenadine syrup, fresh lime juice, and Angostura bitters.
Stir the ingredients well to ensure they are thoroughly mixed.
Chill the rum punch in the refrigerator for at least 1-2 hours to allow the flavors to meld.
Just before serving, fill glasses with ice cubes.
Pour the chilled Caribbean Rum Punch over the ice in each glass.
Garnish with pineapple slices, orange slices, and maraschino cherries.
Stir each glass gently before serving to mix the flavors.
Optionally, you can add more grenadine for color and sweetness if desired.
Serve the Caribbean Rum Punch at your tropical gathering or enjoy it on a sunny day.

This delicious cocktail captures the spirit of the Caribbean with its fruity and tropical flavors. Remember to enjoy responsibly!

Bajan Flying Fish Cutter

Ingredients:

- Fresh flying fish fillets
- Bajan seasoning (a mixture of herbs and spices, including thyme, marjoram, garlic, onion, salt, and pepper)
- Flour (for coating the fish)
- Vegetable oil (for frying)
- Bajan hot pepper sauce
- Bajan salt bread or a roll (cutter)

Instructions:

Clean and season the flying fish fillets with the Bajan seasoning. Allow them to marinate for at least 30 minutes to let the flavors penetrate the fish.
Coat the seasoned fish fillets with flour, shaking off any excess.
Heat vegetable oil in a frying pan over medium heat.
Fry the flying fish fillets until they are golden brown and cooked through. This usually takes a few minutes on each side, depending on the thickness of the fillets.
Once the fish is cooked, remove it from the pan and let it drain on paper towels to absorb any excess oil.
Slice the Bajan salt bread or roll in half, creating a pocket for the fish.
Place the fried flying fish fillets into the bread or roll and add Bajan hot pepper sauce to taste.
Serve your Bajan Flying Fish Cutter hot and enjoy the delicious combination of crispy fish and flavorful Bajan spices.

This dish is not only a beloved local delicacy in Barbados but also a representation of the island's culinary heritage. The Bajan Flying Fish Cutter is often enjoyed as a quick and tasty snack or as a part of a larger meal.

Plantain Chips

Ingredients:

- Green or yellow plantains (firm, not overly ripe)
- Vegetable oil for frying
- Salt (optional, for seasoning)

Instructions:

Peel the plantains: Cut off the ends of the plantains and make a shallow slit along the length of each plantain. Carefully peel the plantains by lifting the skin with your fingers or a knife.
Slice the plantains: Using a sharp knife or a mandoline slicer, cut the peeled plantains into thin, even slices. Aim for slices that are about 1/8 to 1/16 inch thick.
Heat the oil: In a deep pan or a fryer, heat vegetable oil to around 350-375°F (175-190°C).
Fry the plantain slices: Carefully add the plantain slices to the hot oil in small batches to avoid overcrowding. Fry until the slices are golden brown and crispy, which usually takes 2-4 minutes per batch.
Remove and drain: Once the plantain chips are golden brown, use a slotted spoon or tongs to remove them from the hot oil. Place the chips on a paper towel-lined plate to drain excess oil.
Season (optional): While the plantain chips are still warm, you can sprinkle them with salt or your favorite seasoning to add extra flavor.
Let them cool: Allow the plantain chips to cool completely before serving to ensure they become crispy.

Enjoy your homemade plantain chips as a delicious and satisfying snack. They can be served on their own or paired with dips like guacamole, salsa, or your favorite sauce. Plantain chips are not only tasty but also a great way to experience the unique flavor and texture of plantains.

Johnny Cakes

Ingredients:

- 2 cups all-purpose flour
- 2 teaspoons baking powder
- 1/2 teaspoon salt
- 2 tablespoons sugar (optional)
- 1/4 cup unsalted butter, cold and cubed
- 2/3 cup milk (you can use water or coconut milk for added flavor)

Instructions:

In a large mixing bowl, combine the flour, baking powder, salt, and sugar (if using).
Add the cold, cubed butter to the dry ingredients. Use your fingers or a pastry cutter to incorporate the butter into the flour mixture until it resembles coarse crumbs.
Slowly add the milk to the mixture, stirring continuously until the dough comes together. You may need to adjust the amount of liquid depending on the consistency of the dough.
Turn the dough out onto a floured surface and knead it lightly for a few minutes until it forms a smooth ball.
Divide the dough into golf ball-sized portions and flatten each portion into a disk or round shape.
Heat a skillet or griddle over medium heat and lightly grease it with oil or butter.
Cook the Johnny Cakes in the skillet for 3-5 minutes on each side or until they are golden brown and cooked through.
Remove the Johnny Cakes from the skillet and let them cool slightly before serving.

Johnny Cakes can be enjoyed on their own or served with various accompaniments such as butter, jam, honey, or as a side dish with savory meals. The texture can range from soft and fluffy to slightly denser, depending on personal preference and regional variations.

Pepper Pot Soup

Ingredients:

- 2 lbs cassava, peeled and diced
- 1 lb eddoes (taro root), peeled and diced
- 1 lb dasheen (or yams), peeled and diced
- 1 lb spinach or callaloo, chopped
- 1 lb salted beef or pork (traditionally, "cassareep" is used to preserve the meat)
- 1 onion, chopped
- 4 cloves garlic, minced
- 2-3 wiri wiri peppers or Scotch bonnet peppers, minced (adjust to taste for spice)
- 1 cinnamon stick
- 4 cloves
- 4 cups coconut milk
- Salt and pepper to taste

Instructions:

Prepare the Meat:
- If using salted meat, soak it in water overnight to reduce the salt content. Rinse and cut into bite-sized pieces.

Cook the Meat:
- In a large pot, combine the meat, onion, garlic, cinnamon stick, and cloves.
- Add enough water to cover the meat and bring it to a boil.
- Reduce the heat to a simmer and cook until the meat is tender.

Add the Root Vegetables:
- Add the diced cassava, eddoes, and dasheen to the pot.
- Cook until the root vegetables are tender.

Add Spinach or Callaloo:
- Stir in the chopped spinach or callaloo and cook until wilted.

Spice it Up:
- Add minced wiri wiri peppers or Scotch bonnet peppers for heat. Adjust the amount based on your spice preference.

Pour in Coconut Milk:
- Pour in the coconut milk, and bring the soup to a gentle simmer. Be careful not to let it boil vigorously.

Season and Serve:
- Season the soup with salt and pepper to taste.

- Remove the cinnamon stick and cloves before serving.

Guyanese Pepper Pot Soup is often served with traditional "cassava bread" or another type of bread. The combination of root vegetables, meat, and aromatic spices creates a rich and satisfying soup with a distinctive Caribbean flavor.

Grilled Snapper

Ingredients:

- Whole snapper or snapper fillets
- Olive oil
- Lemon juice
- Garlic, minced
- Fresh herbs (such as parsley, thyme, or rosemary), chopped
- Salt and black pepper to taste
- Optional: red pepper flakes for a bit of heat

Instructions:

Prepare the Snapper:
- If using a whole snapper, make sure it is cleaned and scaled. You can ask your fishmonger to do this for you.
- Pat the fish dry with paper towels.

Make the Marinade:
- In a bowl, mix olive oil, lemon juice, minced garlic, chopped fresh herbs, salt, black pepper, and red pepper flakes (if using). Adjust the quantities to your taste preferences.

Marinate the Snapper:
- Rub the snapper, both inside and out, with the marinade. Ensure the marinade gets into the cavities and cuts of the fish for maximum flavor.
- Allow the snapper to marinate for at least 30 minutes, or refrigerate for a few hours for more intense flavor.

Preheat the Grill:
- Preheat your grill to medium-high heat. Make sure the grates are clean and lightly oiled to prevent sticking.

Grill the Snapper:
- Place the marinated snapper on the preheated grill. If using fillets, you can use a grilling basket or wrap the fillets in aluminum foil to prevent them from falling apart.

Cooking Time:
- Grill the snapper for about 4-6 minutes per side, depending on the thickness of the fish. The internal temperature should reach 145°F (63°C) for the fish to be fully cooked.

Baste with Marinade:
- Occasionally baste the snapper with the remaining marinade during the grilling process to keep it moist and flavorful.

Check for Doneness:
- The fish is done when it flakes easily with a fork and has a nicely charred exterior.

Serve:
- Carefully transfer the grilled snapper to a serving platter. Garnish with additional fresh herbs and lemon wedges.

Grilled snapper pairs well with a variety of side dishes such as grilled vegetables, rice, or a fresh salad. It's a simple and delightful way to enjoy the natural flavors of the fish with the added smokiness from the grill.

Caribbean Coleslaw

Ingredients:

- 1 small green cabbage, shredded
- 1 large carrot, grated
- 1 cup pineapple, diced
- 1/2 cup mango, diced
- 1/4 cup red bell pepper, finely chopped
- 1/4 cup green onions, sliced
- 1/4 cup fresh cilantro or parsley, chopped

For the Dressing:

- 1/2 cup mayonnaise
- 2 tablespoons plain Greek yogurt
- 2 tablespoons honey
- 2 tablespoons apple cider vinegar
- 1 teaspoon Dijon mustard
- Salt and black pepper to taste

Instructions:

Prepare the Vegetables and Fruits:
- Shred the green cabbage, grate the carrot, dice the pineapple and mango, finely chop the red bell pepper, slice the green onions, and chop the cilantro or parsley.

Combine in a Bowl:
- In a large mixing bowl, combine the shredded cabbage, grated carrot, diced pineapple, diced mango, chopped red bell pepper, sliced green onions, and chopped cilantro or parsley.

Make the Dressing:
- In a separate bowl, whisk together the mayonnaise, Greek yogurt, honey, apple cider vinegar, Dijon mustard, salt, and black pepper. Adjust the sweetness and acidity to your liking.

Mix and Toss:
- Pour the dressing over the vegetables and fruits in the large bowl.

- Toss everything together until the coleslaw is evenly coated with the dressing.

Chill and Marinate:
- Cover the bowl and refrigerate the Caribbean coleslaw for at least 30 minutes to allow the flavors to meld.

Serve:
- Before serving, give the coleslaw a final toss. Adjust the seasoning if necessary.
- Serve the Caribbean coleslaw as a refreshing side dish at your next barbecue, picnic, or alongside grilled meats or seafood.

This Caribbean coleslaw adds a tropical twist to the traditional coleslaw, making it a perfect accompaniment to Caribbean-inspired dishes or any meal where you want a burst of flavors and colors.

Guava BBQ Ribs

Ingredients:

- 2 racks of baby back ribs
- Salt and black pepper to season the ribs

For the Guava BBQ Sauce:

- 1 cup guava jelly or guava paste
- 1/2 cup ketchup
- 1/4 cup soy sauce
- 1/4 cup apple cider vinegar
- 1/4 cup brown sugar
- 2 cloves garlic, minced
- 1 teaspoon Dijon mustard
- 1 teaspoon smoked paprika
- 1/2 teaspoon ground cumin
- 1/2 teaspoon onion powder
- 1/4 teaspoon cayenne pepper (adjust to taste)
- Salt and black pepper to taste

Instructions:

Prepare the Ribs:
- Remove the membrane from the back of the ribs if it's still attached. Season the ribs generously with salt and black pepper.

Preheat the Grill:
- Preheat your grill to medium-high heat for both direct and indirect grilling.

Grill the Ribs:
- Place the seasoned ribs on the grill over indirect heat. Grill for about 2 to 2.5 hours or until the ribs are tender. You can use a meat thermometer to ensure the internal temperature reaches at least 145°F (63°C).

Make the Guava BBQ Sauce:
- In a saucepan over medium heat, combine guava jelly, ketchup, soy sauce, apple cider vinegar, brown sugar, minced garlic, Dijon mustard, smoked paprika, ground cumin, onion powder, cayenne pepper, salt, and black pepper.

- Simmer the sauce for about 15-20 minutes, stirring occasionally, until it thickens and develops a rich flavor.

Glaze the Ribs:
- During the last 15-20 minutes of grilling, baste the ribs with the guava BBQ sauce, turning and glazing them every 5 minutes until the ribs are nicely coated and caramelized.

Rest and Serve:
- Once the ribs are done, let them rest for a few minutes before slicing.
- Serve the Guava BBQ Ribs with extra sauce on the side for dipping.

This recipe combines the tenderness of grilled ribs with the tropical sweetness of guava, creating a delightful and memorable dish perfect for a backyard barbecue or any special occasion.

Sorrel Drink

Ingredients:

- 2 cups dried sorrel petals (hibiscus petals)
- 8-10 cups water
- 1 to 2 cups sugar (adjust to taste)
- 1-2 inches of ginger, peeled and sliced
- 5-6 cloves
- 1-2 cinnamon sticks
- Optional: orange peel or zest for additional flavor
- Optional: a splash of rum or wine for an adult version

Instructions:

Rinse the Sorrel Petals:
- Rinse the dried sorrel petals under cold running water to remove any dust or debris.

Boil the Sorrel:
- In a large pot, bring the water to a boil. Once boiling, add the rinsed sorrel petals, ginger slices, cloves, and cinnamon sticks.

Simmer:
- Reduce the heat to low and let the mixture simmer for about 15-20 minutes. This allows the sorrel petals to infuse their flavor into the water.

Sweeten the Mixture:
- Add sugar to the pot, stirring until it dissolves. Adjust the amount of sugar according to your sweetness preference.

Strain and Cool:
- Remove the pot from heat and strain the liquid to separate the sorrel petals and spices. Allow the liquid to cool to room temperature.

Chill:
- Once the sorrel drink has cooled, refrigerate it for at least a few hours or overnight. Chilling enhances the flavors.

Serve:
- Serve the sorrel drink over ice and garnish with a slice of orange or a twist of orange peel if desired.
- For an adult version, you can add a splash of rum or wine to the individual servings.

Sorrel drink is not only refreshing but also known for its potential health benefits. It is rich in antioxidants and vitamin C. Enjoyed cold, this beverage is a delightful and festive addition to celebrations or as a cooling drink on a warm day.

Stewed Oxtail

Ingredients:

- 3-4 pounds oxtail, cut into sections
- Salt and black pepper to taste
- 2 tablespoons vegetable oil
- 1 large onion, diced
- 4 cloves garlic, minced
- 2 carrots, peeled and sliced
- 2 celery stalks, chopped
- 2 tomatoes, diced
- 1 tablespoon tomato paste
- 1 tablespoon all-purpose flour
- 2 cups beef broth
- 1 cup red wine (optional)
- 2 bay leaves
- 1 teaspoon dried thyme
- 1 teaspoon paprika
- 1 teaspoon Worcestershire sauce
- Chopped fresh parsley for garnish (optional)

Instructions:

Prepare the Oxtail:
- Season the oxtail sections with salt and black pepper.

Brown the Oxtail:
- Heat vegetable oil in a large, heavy-bottomed pot or Dutch oven over medium-high heat. Brown the oxtail pieces on all sides until they are well-seared. Work in batches if necessary to avoid overcrowding the pot.

Sauté Vegetables:
- Add diced onion, minced garlic, sliced carrots, and chopped celery to the pot. Sauté the vegetables until they are softened.

Add Tomatoes and Tomato Paste:
- Stir in diced tomatoes and tomato paste. Cook for a few minutes to allow the tomatoes to break down and the flavors to meld.

Thicken the Stew:

- Sprinkle flour over the ingredients and stir well to combine. This helps thicken the stew.

Pour in Broth and Wine:
- Pour in beef broth and red wine (if using), scraping the bottom of the pot to release any flavorful bits. Add bay leaves, dried thyme, paprika, and Worcestershire sauce.

Simmer:
- Bring the stew to a boil, then reduce the heat to low. Cover the pot and let it simmer for 2.5 to 3 hours or until the oxtail is tender. Stir occasionally and add more broth or water if needed.

Check Seasoning:
- Taste and adjust the seasoning if necessary.

Serve:
- Discard the bay leaves before serving. Garnish with chopped fresh parsley if desired.

Stewed oxtail is often served over rice, mashed potatoes, or with bread to soak up the flavorful sauce. This dish is rich and comforting, making it a favorite in many culinary traditions.

Sweet Potato Pudding

Ingredients:

- 4 cups grated sweet potatoes (about 4 medium-sized sweet potatoes)
- 1 cup grated coconut (fresh or desiccated, unsweetened)
- 1 cup all-purpose flour
- 2 cups brown sugar
- 1 teaspoon ground cinnamon
- 1/2 teaspoon ground nutmeg
- 1/2 teaspoon ground ginger
- 1/4 teaspoon salt
- 1 cup coconut milk
- 1 cup water
- 1 teaspoon vanilla extract
- 1 cup raisins (optional)
- Butter or oil (for greasing the baking dish)

Instructions:

Preheat the Oven:
- Preheat your oven to 350°F (175°C). Grease a baking dish with butter or oil.

Prepare the Sweet Potatoes and Coconut:
- Peel and grate the sweet potatoes. Grate the coconut if using fresh, or measure out the desiccated coconut.

Combine Dry Ingredients:
- In a large mixing bowl, combine the grated sweet potatoes, grated coconut, all-purpose flour, brown sugar, ground cinnamon, ground nutmeg, ground ginger, and salt. Mix well to ensure even distribution of the dry ingredients.

Add Wet Ingredients:
- In a separate bowl, combine the coconut milk, water, and vanilla extract. Gradually add this mixture to the dry ingredients, stirring to create a thick batter.

Optional: Add Raisins:
- If you're using raisins, fold them into the batter at this point.

Pour into Baking Dish:

- Pour the batter into the greased baking dish, spreading it out evenly.

Bake:
- Bake in the preheated oven for approximately 1.5 to 2 hours or until the pudding is set and a toothpick inserted into the center comes out clean.

Cool and Serve:
- Allow the sweet potato pudding to cool in the baking dish before cutting it into squares or slices.
- Serve the pudding warm or at room temperature.

Sweet potato pudding is often enjoyed on its own, but it can also be served with a scoop of ice cream, a dollop of whipped cream, or a drizzle of caramel sauce for added indulgence. This dessert is a wonderful way to showcase the flavors of sweet potatoes and coconut in a comforting and satisfying treat.

Pigeon Peas and Rice

Ingredients:

- 2 cups long-grain rice
- 1 cup canned pigeon peas (gandules) or cooked dried pigeon peas
- 1 can (about 14 ounces) coconut milk
- 2 cups water
- 1 onion, finely chopped
- 2 cloves garlic, minced
- 1 bell pepper, diced (any color)
- 1 medium tomato, diced
- 2 sprigs thyme
- 2 tablespoons vegetable oil
- 1 teaspoon ground cumin
- 1 teaspoon paprika
- Salt and pepper to taste

Instructions:

Prepare the Rice and Pigeon Peas:
- Rinse the rice under cold water until the water runs clear.
- If using canned pigeon peas, drain and rinse them. If using dried pigeon peas, ensure they are cooked and ready for use.

Sauté Aromatics:
- In a large pot or Dutch oven, heat the vegetable oil over medium heat. Add chopped onion, minced garlic, and diced bell pepper. Sauté until the vegetables are softened.

Add Tomatoes and Spices:
- Stir in the diced tomatoes, ground cumin, paprika, thyme sprigs, salt, and pepper. Cook for a few minutes until the tomatoes break down and the spices release their flavors.

Add Rice and Pigeon Peas:
- Add the rinsed rice and canned or cooked pigeon peas to the pot. Stir well to coat the rice and peas with the aromatic mixture.

Pour in Coconut Milk and Water:
- Pour in the coconut milk and water. Stir the mixture thoroughly to combine all the ingredients.

Bring to a Boil and Simmer:

- Bring the mixture to a boil, then reduce the heat to low. Cover the pot and let it simmer for about 18-20 minutes or until the rice is cooked and the liquid is absorbed.

Fluff and Serve:
- Once the rice is cooked, fluff it with a fork to separate the grains. Remove the thyme sprigs before serving.

Serve Warm:
- Pigeon peas and rice can be served as a side dish or as a main course. It pairs well with grilled or stewed meats and adds a flavorful touch to any Caribbean-inspired meal.

This dish not only offers a wonderful blend of textures and flavors but also showcases the vibrant and aromatic elements of Caribbean cuisine.

Bammy (Cassava Flatbread)

Ingredients:

- 2 cups cassava flour (also known as yuca or manioc flour)
- 1/2 teaspoon salt
- 1 cup water (approximately)
- Coconut oil or butter (for greasing)

Instructions:

Prepare the Cassava Flour:
- In a large mixing bowl, combine the cassava flour and salt.

Add Water:
- Gradually add water to the cassava flour while mixing continuously. Continue to mix until the dough comes together. You may need more or less water depending on the specific cassava flour you're using.

Knead the Dough:
- Knead the dough on a floured surface for a few minutes until it becomes smooth. The texture should be soft but not sticky.

Shape the Bammy:
- Divide the dough into small portions and shape each portion into a round, flat disc. Typically, bammy is about 4-6 inches in diameter and 1/4 to 1/2 inch thick.

Cook the Bammy:
- Heat a griddle or skillet over medium-high heat. Grease it lightly with coconut oil or butter.
- Place the shaped bammy on the griddle and cook for about 5-7 minutes on each side or until golden brown. You can also bake the bammy in the oven at 350°F (175°C) for about 20-25 minutes, flipping halfway through.

Serve:
- Once cooked, the bammy should have a slightly crispy exterior and a soft interior. Serve it hot with fried fish or your choice of protein.

Bammy is a versatile bread that can be enjoyed with various toppings or accompaniments. It's a staple in Jamaican cuisine and is especially popular with seafood dishes. If you're looking to experience authentic Caribbean flavors, trying bammy with fried fish is a delicious and classic combination.

Black Cake

Ingredients:

- 2 cups mixed dried fruits (raisins, currants, prunes, cherries, etc.)
- 1 cup rum (dark rum is commonly used)
- 1 cup butter, softened
- 1 cup brown sugar
- 6 large eggs
- 2 cups all-purpose flour
- 1 teaspoon baking powder
- 1 teaspoon ground cinnamon
- 1/2 teaspoon ground nutmeg
- 1/2 teaspoon allspice
- 1/4 teaspoon salt
- 1 cup browning (burnt sugar)*
- 1 cup breadcrumbs
- 1/2 cup ground almonds or almond meal
- 1 teaspoon vanilla extract

Instructions:

Prepare the Fruits:
- Place the mixed dried fruits in a bowl and pour the rum over them. Allow the fruits to soak, preferably overnight or for at least a few hours.

Preheat the Oven:
- Preheat your oven to 325°F (163°C). Grease and line a cake pan with parchment paper.

Cream Butter and Sugar:
- In a large mixing bowl, cream together the softened butter and brown sugar until light and fluffy.

Add Eggs:
- Add the eggs one at a time, beating well after each addition.

Combine Dry Ingredients:
- In a separate bowl, whisk together the flour, baking powder, cinnamon, nutmeg, allspice, and salt.

Add Flour Mixture:

- Gradually add the dry ingredients to the creamed butter and sugar, mixing well.

Add Browning, Breadcrumbs, and Almonds:
- Stir in the browning (burnt sugar), breadcrumbs, and ground almonds.

Fold in Soaked Fruits:
- Fold in the soaked dried fruits and any remaining rum from the soaking process.

Add Vanilla Extract:
- Stir in the vanilla extract.

Pour into Pan:
- Pour the batter into the prepared cake pan, spreading it evenly.

Bake:
- Bake in the preheated oven for about 1.5 to 2 hours or until a toothpick inserted into the center comes out clean. The baking time may vary, so keep an eye on the cake and adjust accordingly.

Cool and Soak (Optional):
- Allow the cake to cool in the pan for a bit before transferring it to a wire rack to cool completely. Some people like to soak the baked cake with additional rum for added moisture and flavor.

Black Cake is often enjoyed during festive occasions, particularly Christmas. It is a labor of love, and families may have their own variations of the recipe, passed down through generations. The result is a flavorful and decadent cake with a unique Caribbean twist.

Curry Shrimp

Ingredients:

- 1 pound (about 500g) large shrimp, peeled and deveined
- 2 tablespoons curry powder
- 1 teaspoon turmeric powder
- 1 teaspoon cumin
- 1 teaspoon coriander
- 1/2 teaspoon chili powder (adjust to taste)
- Salt and black pepper to taste
- 2 tablespoons vegetable oil or ghee
- 1 onion, finely chopped
- 3 cloves garlic, minced
- 1-inch piece of ginger, grated
- 1 cup tomatoes, diced
- 1 cup coconut milk
- Fresh cilantro for garnish (optional)
- Lemon or lime wedges for serving

Instructions:

Prepare the Shrimp:
- Clean, peel, and devein the shrimp. Pat them dry with paper towels.

Mix the Spices:
- In a bowl, combine the curry powder, turmeric, cumin, coriander, chili powder, salt, and black pepper. Mix the spices well.

Season the Shrimp:
- Toss the shrimp in the spice mixture, ensuring they are well coated. Allow them to marinate for at least 15-30 minutes.

Cook the Shrimp:
- In a large skillet or pan, heat the vegetable oil or ghee over medium heat. Add the chopped onion and sauté until softened.

Add Aromatics:
- Add the minced garlic and grated ginger to the pan. Sauté for about 1-2 minutes until fragrant.

Cook Shrimp:

- Add the marinated shrimp to the pan and cook for 2-3 minutes on each side or until they turn pink and opaque.

Add Tomatoes:
- Stir in the diced tomatoes and cook for an additional 2 minutes until they begin to soften.

Pour Coconut Milk:
- Pour in the coconut milk, stirring to combine. Allow the curry to simmer for 5-7 minutes, letting the flavors meld and the sauce thicken slightly.

Adjust Seasoning:
- Taste and adjust the seasoning if needed. You can add more salt, pepper, or curry powder according to your preferences.

Garnish and Serve:
- Garnish the curry shrimp with fresh cilantro, if desired. Serve the curry shrimp over rice, couscous, or with bread. Optionally, squeeze some lemon or lime juice over the dish before serving.

Curry shrimp is a versatile dish that pairs well with various side dishes. It's a quick and delicious way to enjoy the bold flavors of curry with succulent shrimp.

Jamaican Patty

Ingredients:

For the Pastry:

- 3 cups all-purpose flour
- 1 teaspoon turmeric (for color)
- 1 teaspoon salt
- 1 cup cold unsalted butter, cut into small cubes
- 1/2 cup cold water (approx.)

For the Filling:

- 1 lb ground beef
- 1 large onion, finely chopped
- 2 cloves garlic, minced
- 1 scallion, finely chopped
- 1 teaspoon thyme
- 1 teaspoon curry powder
- 1 teaspoon paprika
- 1/2 teaspoon cayenne pepper (adjust to taste)
- Salt and black pepper to taste
- 1/4 cup breadcrumbs
- 1/2 cup beef broth or water
- 2 tablespoons vegetable oil for cooking

Instructions:

For the Pastry:

In a large bowl, combine the flour, turmeric, and salt.
Add the cold butter cubes and use your fingers to rub the butter into the flour until it resembles coarse crumbs.
Gradually add the cold water, mixing until the dough comes together. Be careful not to overmix.
Form the dough into a ball, wrap it in plastic wrap, and refrigerate for at least 30 minutes.

For the Filling:

In a skillet, heat vegetable oil over medium heat. Add chopped onions, garlic, and scallions. Sauté until softened.
Add ground beef to the skillet and cook until browned.
Stir in thyme, curry powder, paprika, cayenne pepper, salt, and black pepper. Cook for a few minutes.
Add breadcrumbs and beef broth (or water) to the meat mixture. Simmer until the liquid is mostly absorbed, creating a flavorful filling.

Assembling and Baking:

Preheat your oven to 375°F (190°C).
Roll out the chilled pastry on a floured surface to about 1/8 inch thickness.
Cut out circles (about 5-6 inches in diameter) using a round cutter or a bowl as a guide.
Place a spoonful of the beef filling onto one half of each pastry circle.
Fold the pastry over the filling to create a half-moon shape. Seal the edges by pressing with a fork or by crimping with your fingers.
Place the patties on a baking sheet lined with parchment paper.
Bake in the preheated oven for 20-25 minutes or until the pastry is golden brown.

Jamaican patties can be enjoyed as a snack or a meal, and they are often served with hot pepper sauce for an extra kick. They're not only delicious but also a delightful representation of Jamaican culinary culture.

Cucumber Chutney

Ingredients:

- 2 medium-sized cucumbers, peeled and finely diced
- 1 small red onion, finely chopped
- 1/2 cup red bell pepper, finely diced
- 1/2 cup green bell pepper, finely diced
- 1/4 cup fresh cilantro (coriander), chopped
- 2 tablespoons fresh mint leaves, chopped
- 1-2 green chilies, finely chopped (adjust to taste)
- 1 teaspoon mustard seeds
- 1/2 teaspoon cumin seeds
- 1/2 teaspoon fennel seeds
- 1/2 teaspoon turmeric powder
- 1/2 teaspoon red chili powder (adjust to taste)
- 1/4 teaspoon asafoetida (hing)
- 1/4 cup white vinegar
- 2 tablespoons olive oil or vegetable oil
- Salt to taste
- 2-3 tablespoons sugar or honey (adjust to taste)

Instructions:

Prepare Cucumbers:
- Peel the cucumbers and finely dice them. Place the diced cucumbers in a bowl and sprinkle a little salt over them. Let them sit for about 15 minutes to release excess water. After 15 minutes, drain the excess water.

Toast Seeds:
- In a small pan, toast mustard seeds, cumin seeds, and fennel seeds until they start to pop and release their aroma. Remove from heat and let them cool.

Combine Ingredients:
- In a large mixing bowl, combine the diced cucumbers, chopped red onion, red and green bell peppers, cilantro, mint leaves, and green chilies.

Add Toasted Seeds and Spices:
- Add the toasted mustard seeds, cumin seeds, and fennel seeds to the bowl. Also, add turmeric powder, red chili powder, and asafoetida.

Mix and Season:
- Mix the ingredients well. Season the mixture with salt to taste.

Prepare Dressing:
- In a small bowl, whisk together white vinegar, olive oil, and sugar (or honey). Adjust the sweetness according to your preference.

Combine and Chill:
- Pour the dressing over the cucumber mixture and toss everything together until well coated. Refrigerate the chutney for at least 30 minutes to allow the flavors to meld.

Serve:
- Serve chilled cucumber chutney as a side dish with grilled meats, sandwiches, or snacks. It adds a refreshing and tangy kick to various dishes.

Cucumber chutney is a versatile condiment that brings a burst of freshness and flavor to your meals. Feel free to adjust the spice levels, sweetness, or add other herbs to suit your taste preferences.

Green Fig and Saltfish

Ingredients:

- 4 green bananas (green figs), peeled and sliced
- 1/2 pound salted codfish, soaked and flaked
- 1 onion, finely chopped
- 2 cloves garlic, minced
- 1 bell pepper (any color), chopped
- 2 tomatoes, diced
- 1/4 cup chopped fresh parsley or cilantro
- 2 tablespoons vegetable oil
- 1 teaspoon thyme
- 1 teaspoon black pepper
- Scotch bonnet pepper or hot sauce (optional, for heat)
- Lime wedges for serving

Instructions:

Peel and slice the green bananas. Boil them in salted water until tender but still firm. Drain and set aside.

Soak the salted codfish in water for a few hours or overnight, changing the water a few times to remove excess salt. Flake the codfish into small pieces.

In a large skillet, heat vegetable oil over medium heat. Add chopped onion, garlic, and bell pepper. Sauté until softened.

Add flaked saltfish to the skillet and cook for a few minutes, stirring to combine.

Add sliced green bananas, diced tomatoes, thyme, and black pepper. Cook until everything is heated through.

If you like it spicy, add finely chopped Scotch bonnet pepper or a few dashes of hot sauce.

Garnish with chopped fresh parsley or cilantro.

Serve hot with lime wedges on the side.

Both cucumber chutney and green fig and saltfish are flavorful and showcase the vibrant and diverse culinary traditions of the Caribbean. Enjoy these dishes as part of a delicious and culturally rich meal!

Barbados Cou-Cou

Ingredients:

- 1 cup cornmeal
- 2 cups okra, finely chopped or grated
- 1 onion, finely chopped
- 2 cloves garlic, minced
- 1 sprig thyme
- 2 cups water or fish broth
- 1 cup coconut milk
- Salt and pepper to taste
- 2 tablespoons butter or margarine (optional)

Instructions:

Prepare Okra:
- Finely chop or grate the okra. If using fresh okra, make sure to remove the stems and tips.

Combine Okra and Cornmeal:
- In a mixing bowl, combine the cornmeal and chopped/grated okra.

Prepare Thyme, Onion, and Garlic:
- Finely chop the onion, mince the garlic, and remove the thyme leaves from the sprig.

Cook Okra and Cornmeal Mixture:
- In a deep saucepan or pot, combine the water or fish broth, coconut milk, chopped onion, minced garlic, and thyme leaves. Bring it to a gentle simmer over medium heat.
- Gradually whisk in the cornmeal and okra mixture, stirring continuously to avoid lumps.

Continue Cooking:
- Lower the heat and continue to stir the mixture, ensuring it remains smooth.
- Cook on low heat for 20-25 minutes or until the cou-cou has a smooth and creamy consistency. Stir frequently to prevent sticking.

Season:
- Season the cou-cou with salt and pepper to taste. Adjust the seasoning according to your preference.

Add Butter (Optional):
- If desired, add butter or margarine to the cou-cou and stir until it melts.

Serve:
- Once the cou-cou reaches the desired consistency, remove it from the heat.
- Serve the cou-cou alongside fish stew, grilled fish, or any other main dish of your choice.

Barbados Cou-Cou is a delicious and comforting dish with a unique texture and flavor. It's an essential part of Bajan cuisine and is often enjoyed as a traditional accompaniment to fish dishes.

Pineapple Ginger Chicken

Ingredients:

- 1.5 lbs (about 700g) boneless, skinless chicken thighs or breasts, cut into bite-sized pieces
- 1 cup pineapple chunks (fresh or canned)
- 1/4 cup soy sauce
- 2 tablespoons honey
- 1 tablespoon rice vinegar
- 1 tablespoon grated fresh ginger
- 2 cloves garlic, minced
- 1 tablespoon cornstarch
- 1/4 cup water
- 2 tablespoons vegetable oil
- Salt and black pepper to taste
- Red pepper flakes (optional, for heat)
- Fresh cilantro or green onions for garnish (optional)
- Cooked rice for serving

Instructions:

Marinate the Chicken:
- In a bowl, combine soy sauce, honey, rice vinegar, grated ginger, minced garlic, and a pinch of black pepper. Stir well to create the marinade.
- Place the chicken pieces in the marinade, ensuring they are well-coated. Allow it to marinate for at least 30 minutes, or you can refrigerate it for a few hours for more flavor.

Prepare Cornstarch Slurry:
- In a small bowl, mix cornstarch with water to create a slurry. This will be used later to thicken the sauce.

Cook the Chicken:
- Heat vegetable oil in a large skillet or wok over medium-high heat.
- Remove chicken from the marinade, allowing excess marinade to drip off. Reserve the marinade for the sauce.
- Add chicken pieces to the hot skillet and cook until browned on all sides and cooked through.

Prepare the Sauce:
- While the chicken is cooking, combine the reserved marinade with the cornstarch slurry.

- Pour the sauce mixture into the skillet with the cooked chicken.

Add Pineapple:
- Add pineapple chunks to the skillet. Stir well to coat the chicken and pineapple with the sauce.
- If you like it spicy, you can add red pepper flakes at this point for some heat.

Simmer:
- Allow the mixture to simmer for a few minutes until the sauce thickens and coats the chicken and pineapple evenly.

Check Seasoning:
- Taste and adjust the seasoning if needed. Add salt or extra soy sauce according to your preference.

Serve:
- Serve the pineapple ginger chicken over cooked rice.
- Garnish with fresh cilantro or green onions if desired.

This Pineapple Ginger Chicken is a delightful combination of sweet and savory flavors with a hint of spiciness. It's a quick and tasty dish that can be enjoyed with steamed rice or your favorite side.

Creole Fish

Ingredients:

- 4 fish fillets (such as snapper, grouper, or tilapia)
- 2 tablespoons olive oil
- 1 onion, finely chopped
- 1 bell pepper (any color), diced
- 2 cloves garlic, minced
- 1 can (about 14 ounces) diced tomatoes, undrained
- 1 tablespoon tomato paste
- 1 teaspoon Creole or Cajun seasoning (adjust to taste)
- 1 teaspoon dried thyme
- 1 teaspoon paprika
- 1/2 teaspoon dried oregano
- Salt and black pepper to taste
- 1/4 teaspoon cayenne pepper (optional, for heat)
- 1/2 cup chicken or vegetable broth
- Fresh parsley or green onions for garnish
- Cooked rice for serving

Instructions:

Season the Fish:
- Season the fish fillets with salt, black pepper, and half of the Creole or Cajun seasoning. Set aside.

Sauté Aromatics:
- In a large skillet, heat olive oil over medium heat. Add chopped onion, diced bell pepper, and minced garlic. Sauté until the vegetables are softened.

Add Tomatoes and Tomato Paste:
- Stir in the diced tomatoes (with their juice) and tomato paste. Cook for a few minutes until the tomatoes break down and the mixture thickens.

Season the Sauce:
- Add the remaining Creole or Cajun seasoning, dried thyme, paprika, dried oregano, salt, black pepper, and cayenne pepper (if using). Stir to combine.

Add Broth:
- Pour in the chicken or vegetable broth, stirring to create a flavorful sauce. Allow the mixture to simmer for a few minutes.

Cook the Fish:

- Gently place the seasoned fish fillets into the skillet, spooning some of the sauce over the top. Cover the skillet and let the fish cook for 8-10 minutes or until it flakes easily with a fork.

Check Seasoning:
- Taste the sauce and adjust the seasoning if needed.

Serve:
- Serve the Creole fish over cooked rice.
- Garnish with fresh parsley or green onions.

Creole fish is a delicious and satisfying dish that brings together bold flavors and a rich, aromatic sauce. It's a wonderful representation of the diverse and flavorful Creole culinary tradition.

Goat Water Stew

Ingredients:

- 2 lbs goat meat, cut into chunks
- 2 tablespoons oil (vegetable or olive oil)
- 1 large onion, chopped
- 3 cloves garlic, minced
- 2 large tomatoes, diced
- 2 bell peppers (any color), chopped
- 2 celery stalks, chopped
- 2 carrots, peeled and sliced
- 1 cup chopped okra
- 2 sprigs thyme
- 2 bay leaves
- 1 teaspoon ground allspice
- 1 teaspoon ground cumin
- 1 teaspoon paprika
- 1 teaspoon curry powder
- Salt and black pepper to taste
- 2 quarts (8 cups) water or beef broth
- 1 cup chopped callaloo or spinach (optional)
- 2-3 potatoes, peeled and diced
- Juice of 1 lime or lemon

Instructions:

Prepare the Goat Meat:
- Rinse the goat meat under cold water and pat it dry with paper towels. Cut it into chunks, removing excess fat if desired.

Season the Goat Meat:
- In a large bowl, season the goat meat with salt, black pepper, ground allspice, cumin, paprika, and curry powder. Toss the meat to ensure it's well-coated with the spices.

Brown the Meat:
- In a large, heavy-bottomed pot or Dutch oven, heat the oil over medium-high heat. Brown the seasoned goat meat in batches, ensuring all sides are seared. Remove the browned meat and set it aside.

Sauté Aromatics:

- In the same pot, add chopped onion and minced garlic. Sauté until the onions are translucent.

Add Vegetables and Spices:
- Add diced tomatoes, chopped bell peppers, chopped celery, sliced carrots, chopped okra, thyme sprigs, bay leaves, and the browned goat meat back into the pot. Stir to combine.

Pour in Water or Broth:
- Pour in the water or beef broth, ensuring it covers the ingredients in the pot. Bring the stew to a boil.

Simmer:
- Reduce the heat to low, cover the pot, and let the stew simmer for at least 2 to 2.5 hours, or until the goat meat is tender.

Add Callaloo/Spinach and Potatoes:
- About 30 minutes before the stew is done, add chopped callaloo or spinach (if using) and diced potatoes. Continue to simmer until the potatoes are cooked through.

Adjust Seasoning:
- Taste the stew and adjust the seasoning if necessary. You can add more salt, pepper, or spices according to your preference.

Finish with Citrus Juice:
- Just before serving, squeeze the juice of one lime or lemon into the stew. This adds a bright and refreshing flavor.

Serve:
- Discard the thyme sprigs and bay leaves before serving. Serve the Goat Water Stew hot, either on its own or with rice or bread.

Goat Water Stew is known for its rich and savory flavor, and it's a beloved dish that reflects the warmth and hospitality of Caribbean cuisine.

Tamarind Balls

Ingredients:

- 1 cup tamarind pulp (without seeds)
- 1 cup granulated sugar
- 1/2 teaspoon ground cinnamon (optional)
- 1/4 teaspoon ground ginger (optional)
- Pinch of salt (optional)
- Additional sugar or chili powder for coating (optional)

Instructions:

Extract Tamarind Pulp:
- Begin by removing the seeds from the tamarind pods. You can do this by breaking the pods open and extracting the sticky pulp. Use your fingers to separate the pulp from the seeds.

Create Tamarind Paste:
- Place the tamarind pulp in a bowl and add a small amount of warm water. Mash the pulp with a spoon or your hands, breaking it down into a thick paste. Discard any remaining seeds.

Sweeten the Tamarind Paste:
- In a saucepan, combine the tamarind paste with granulated sugar. Cook the mixture over low heat, stirring continuously until the sugar dissolves and the tamarind paste thickens. This step helps to reduce the stickiness of the tamarind and makes it easier to form into balls.

Add Spices (Optional):
- If desired, add ground cinnamon, ground ginger, and a pinch of salt to the tamarind-sugar mixture. Stir well to incorporate the spices.

Let it Cool:
- Allow the tamarind mixture to cool until it is comfortable to handle.

Form Tamarind Balls:
- Take small portions of the tamarind mixture and roll them into balls using your hands. The size of the balls is up to your preference.

Coat in Sugar or Spice (Optional):
- Optionally, you can roll the tamarind balls in additional granulated sugar or chili powder for added flavor and texture.

Set and Serve:
- Place the tamarind balls on a plate or tray and let them set at room temperature for a few hours or until they firm up.

Tamarind balls are a delightful combination of sweet, tangy, and sometimes spicy flavors. They make for a unique and enjoyable snack. The addition of spices or coatings can be adjusted to suit your taste preferences. Enjoy these tamarind balls as a sweet treat or a palate-cleansing snack.

Soursop Smoothie

Ingredients:

- 1 cup soursop pulp (fresh or frozen)
- 1 ripe banana, peeled and sliced (for creaminess)
- 1/2 cup Greek yogurt or coconut milk (for creaminess)
- 1/2 cup pineapple chunks (fresh or frozen)
- 1/2 cup mango chunks (fresh or frozen)
- 1-2 tablespoons honey or agave syrup (optional, depending on sweetness preference)
- 1 cup ice cubes
- 1/2 cup water or coconut water

Instructions:

Prepare Soursop Pulp:
- If using fresh soursop, cut it open and remove the seeds. Scoop out the pulp and set it aside. If using frozen soursop, thaw it slightly for easier blending.

Combine Ingredients:
- In a blender, combine the soursop pulp, sliced banana, Greek yogurt or coconut milk, pineapple chunks, mango chunks, honey or agave syrup (if using), ice cubes, and water or coconut water.

Blend Until Smooth:
- Blend the ingredients on high speed until you achieve a smooth and creamy consistency. If the smoothie is too thick, you can add more water or coconut water in small increments until it reaches your desired consistency.

Taste and Adjust:
- Taste the smoothie and adjust the sweetness by adding more honey or agave syrup if needed.

Serve:
- Pour the soursop smoothie into glasses and serve immediately.

Optional Additions and Variations:

- Lime or Lemon Juice: Add a splash of fresh lime or lemon juice for a citrusy kick.
- Mint Leaves: Garnish with fresh mint leaves for a burst of freshness.
- Chia Seeds or Flaxseeds: Boost the nutritional content by adding chia seeds or flaxseeds for added fiber and omega-3 fatty acids.

- Vanilla Extract: Enhance the flavor with a drop or two of vanilla extract.

Soursop smoothies are not only delicious but also packed with vitamins, minerals, and antioxidants. They make a nutritious and satisfying drink that can be enjoyed for breakfast, as a snack, or as a refreshing beverage on a hot day.

Fried Dumplings

Ingredients:

- 2 cups all-purpose flour
- 1 teaspoon baking powder
- 1/2 teaspoon salt
- 1 tablespoon sugar (optional, for sweet dumplings)
- 2 tablespoons butter or vegetable shortening
- 3/4 cup milk or water (adjust as needed)
- Oil for frying

Instructions:

Prepare the Dough:
- In a large mixing bowl, combine the all-purpose flour, baking powder, salt, and sugar (if using). Mix well to evenly distribute the dry ingredients.

Add Fat:
- Cut in the butter or vegetable shortening into the dry ingredients until the mixture resembles coarse crumbs.

Form Dough:
- Gradually add the milk or water, a little at a time, and mix until a soft dough forms. You may need more or less liquid depending on the humidity and type of flour used.

Knead the Dough:
- Turn the dough out onto a floured surface and knead it for a few minutes until it becomes smooth and elastic.

Shape Dumplings:
- Pinch off small portions of the dough and shape them into balls or discs, depending on your preference. You can make them the size of golf balls or flatten them slightly for a more traditional shape.

Heat the Oil:
- In a deep skillet or frying pan, heat enough oil to cover the dumplings over medium-high heat. The oil should be hot but not smoking.

Fry the Dumplings:
- Carefully add the shaped dumplings to the hot oil, leaving enough space between them to prevent sticking. Fry until they are golden brown on one side, then flip and brown the other side. This usually takes about 2-4 minutes per side.

Drain and Serve:

- Use a slotted spoon to remove the fried dumplings from the oil and place them on a paper towel-lined plate to drain any excess oil.

Serve Warm:
- Fried dumplings are best served warm. They can be enjoyed on their own, with a dipping sauce, or alongside your favorite savory dish.

Variations:

- Sweet Dumplings: Add more sugar to the dough if you prefer sweet dumplings. They can be served with honey, syrup, or powdered sugar.
- Spiced Dumplings: Add a pinch of cinnamon, nutmeg, or your favorite spices to the dough for a flavorful twist.
- Stuffed Dumplings: Fill the center of each dumpling with a sweet or savory filling before frying.

Fried dumplings are a simple yet satisfying treat that can complement a variety of meals. Experiment with different variations to suit your taste preferences.

Trinidadian Pelau

Ingredients:

- 2 cups chicken pieces (chicken thighs and drumsticks work well)
- 2 cups parboiled rice
- 1 cup pigeon peas (canned or soaked overnight if dried)
- 1 large onion, chopped
- 2 cloves garlic, minced
- 1 sweet pepper (bell pepper), chopped
- 1 large carrot, diced
- 1 cup pumpkin or squash, diced
- 2 sprigs thyme
- 2 cups coconut milk
- 2 tablespoons vegetable oil
- 2 tablespoons brown sugar
- 2 tablespoons soy sauce
- 2 tablespoons ketchup
- 2 tablespoons green seasoning (a Trinidadian herb blend)
- Salt and black pepper to taste
- Scotch bonnet pepper (optional, for heat)
- Chopped green onions or cilantro for garnish

Instructions:

Season and Brown the Chicken:
- In a large pot or Dutch oven, season the chicken pieces with salt, black pepper, green seasoning, soy sauce, and ketchup.
- Heat vegetable oil in the pot over medium heat. Brown the seasoned chicken on all sides.

Caramelize the Sugar:
- Sprinkle brown sugar over the browned chicken and allow it to caramelize. Stir the chicken to coat it evenly with the caramelized sugar.

Add Aromatics:
- Add chopped onion, minced garlic, sweet pepper, and thyme to the pot. Sauté until the vegetables are softened.

Add Vegetables:
- Stir in diced carrot and pumpkin or squash. Cook for a few minutes until the vegetables start to soften.

Add Rice and Pigeon Peas:

- Add parboiled rice and drained pigeon peas to the pot. Mix well with the other ingredients.

Pour in Coconut Milk:
- Pour in the coconut milk and add the Scotch bonnet pepper (whole, for flavor). Stir the ingredients together.

Simmer:
- Allow the mixture to come to a boil, then reduce the heat to low. Cover the pot and let it simmer until the rice is cooked, and the liquid is absorbed. This usually takes about 25-30 minutes.

Check Seasoning:
- Taste the pelau and adjust the seasoning if needed. Add salt or more green seasoning according to your preference.

Finish and Serve:
- Once the rice is cooked, fluff it with a fork, remove the Scotch bonnet pepper, and garnish the pelau with chopped green onions or cilantro.
- Serve the Trinidadian Pelau hot, either on its own or with a side of salad or coleslaw.

Trinidadian Pelau is a delightful and comforting dish that captures the essence of Caribbean flavors. It's often enjoyed at gatherings, celebrations, and family meals.

Avocado Mango Salad

Ingredients:

- 2 ripe avocados, diced
- 1 large mango, peeled, pitted, and diced
- 1/2 red onion, finely chopped
- 1 cup cherry tomatoes, halved
- 1/4 cup fresh cilantro, chopped
- Juice of 1 lime
- 2 tablespoons extra-virgin olive oil
- Salt and black pepper to taste
- Optional: Red chili flakes for a hint of spice

Instructions:

Prepare the Ingredients:
- Peel, pit, and dice the ripe avocados.
- Peel, pit, and dice the mango.
- Finely chop the red onion.
- Halve the cherry tomatoes.
- Chop the fresh cilantro.

Combine the Ingredients:
- In a large salad bowl, combine the diced avocados, diced mango, chopped red onion, halved cherry tomatoes, and chopped cilantro.

Prepare the Dressing:
- In a small bowl, whisk together the lime juice, extra-virgin olive oil, salt, and black pepper. Adjust the seasoning to taste.

Dress the Salad:
- Drizzle the dressing over the avocado and mango mixture.

Gently Toss:
- Gently toss the salad ingredients with the dressing, ensuring that the avocado and mango are evenly coated.

Optional Spice:
- If you like a bit of spice, sprinkle red chili flakes over the salad and toss again.

Chill (Optional):
- You can refrigerate the salad for about 15-30 minutes to allow the flavors to meld and the salad to chill slightly.

Serve:

- Serve the Avocado Mango Salad chilled, garnished with extra cilantro if desired.

Variations:

- Protein Boost: Add grilled shrimp, chicken, or chickpeas for a protein boost.
- Nuts and Seeds: Sprinkle with toasted nuts (such as almonds or walnuts) or seeds (such as sunflower seeds or pumpkin seeds) for added crunch.
- Feta or Goat Cheese: Crumble some feta or goat cheese over the salad for a creamy and tangy touch.

This Avocado Mango Salad is not only visually appealing but also a delightful combination of textures and flavors. It's a great side dish for summer barbecues, picnics, or as a light accompaniment to grilled meats or seafood.

Sea Moss Drink

Ingredients:

- 1/4 cup dried sea moss
- 2 cups water (for soaking sea moss)
- 4 cups water (for blending)
- 1 cinnamon stick (optional)
- 1 teaspoon vanilla extract (optional)
- 1 cup coconut milk or almond milk
- 1/2 cup condensed milk or sweetened condensed coconut milk
- 1/4 cup honey or agave syrup (adjust to taste)
- Nutmeg or cinnamon for garnish (optional)

Instructions:

Prepare Sea Moss:
- Rinse the dried sea moss thoroughly to remove any debris.
- Soak the sea moss in 2 cups of water for at least 4-6 hours or overnight. This helps it rehydrate and soften.

Blend Sea Moss:
- After soaking, the sea moss will have expanded and softened. Rinse it again.
- In a blender, combine the soaked sea moss with 4 cups of water. Add a cinnamon stick if using.
- Blend until you achieve a smooth and gelatinous consistency.

Strain (Optional):
- Strain the blended sea moss mixture using a fine mesh strainer to remove any remaining bits. This step is optional, as some people prefer the added texture.

Combine Ingredients:
- In a separate pot, heat the coconut milk or almond milk over low heat. Add the blended sea moss mixture and stir well.
- If using, add vanilla extract for flavor.

Sweeten the Drink:
- Stir in condensed milk or sweetened condensed coconut milk to sweeten the drink. Adjust the sweetness with honey or agave syrup to taste.

Simmer (Optional):
- Simmer the mixture over low heat for about 10-15 minutes, stirring occasionally. This step is optional but helps to meld the flavors.

Cool and Serve:
- Allow the Sea Moss Drink to cool to room temperature before refrigerating.
- Serve the chilled Sea Moss Drink in glasses, garnished with a sprinkle of nutmeg or cinnamon if desired.

Tips:

- Adjust the sweetness and thickness of the drink according to your taste preferences.
- Experiment with different variations, such as adding spices like nutmeg or cinnamon during blending.

Sea Moss Drink is enjoyed for its potential health benefits and is often consumed for its supposed nutritional properties. Remember to source high-quality sea moss and consult with a healthcare professional if you have any concerns or medical conditions.

Coconut Bread

Ingredients:

- 2 cups all-purpose flour
- 1 cup shredded coconut (sweetened or unsweetened)
- 1 cup sugar
- 1 teaspoon baking powder
- 1/2 teaspoon baking soda
- 1/4 teaspoon salt
- 1 cup coconut milk
- 1/2 cup unsalted butter, melted
- 2 large eggs
- 1 teaspoon vanilla extract

Instructions:

Preheat the Oven:
- Preheat your oven to 350°F (175°C). Grease and flour a standard-sized loaf pan.

Combine Dry Ingredients:
- In a large bowl, whisk together the all-purpose flour, shredded coconut, sugar, baking powder, baking soda, and salt.

Mix Wet Ingredients:
- In a separate bowl, whisk together the coconut milk, melted butter, eggs, and vanilla extract until well combined.

Combine Wet and Dry Mixtures:
- Pour the wet ingredients into the dry ingredients and gently fold them together until just combined. Be careful not to overmix; it's okay if there are a few lumps.

Pour Batter into Loaf Pan:
- Pour the batter into the prepared loaf pan, spreading it evenly.

Bake:
- Bake in the preheated oven for approximately 50-60 minutes or until a toothpick inserted into the center comes out clean.

Cool:
- Allow the coconut bread to cool in the pan for about 10 minutes, then transfer it to a wire rack to cool completely.

Slice and Serve:

- Once the coconut bread has cooled, slice it into pieces and serve. It can be enjoyed on its own or with a spread of butter or cream cheese.

Optional Additions:

- Nuts or Dried Fruit: Add a cup of chopped nuts (such as walnuts or pecans) or dried fruit (such as raisins or dried cranberries) for added texture and flavor.
- Lime or Lemon Zest: For a citrusy twist, add the zest of one lime or lemon to the batter.

This Coconut Bread is a delightful treat with a tropical flair. Its sweet coconut flavor and moist texture make it a favorite for coconut lovers.

Crab and Callaloo Dumplings

Ingredients:

Dumpling Dough:

- 2 cups all-purpose flour
- 1/2 teaspoon salt
- 3/4 cup water (or as needed)
- 1 tablespoon vegetable oil

Filling:

- 1 cup crab meat, cooked and shredded
- 1 cup callaloo, chopped (substitute with spinach if callaloo is not available)
- 1 small onion, finely chopped
- 2 cloves garlic, minced
- 1 tablespoon vegetable oil
- 1 teaspoon thyme leaves
- Salt and black pepper to taste
- Scotch bonnet pepper (optional, for heat)
- 1 tablespoon lime or lemon juice

Instructions:

Prepare Dumpling Dough:

In a large mixing bowl, combine the all-purpose flour and salt.
Gradually add water while kneading the dough until it comes together. Adjust the water as needed to form a soft and smooth dough.
Add vegetable oil to the dough and continue kneading until it becomes elastic.
Cover the dough with a damp cloth and let it rest for about 30 minutes.

Prepare Filling:

In a skillet, heat vegetable oil over medium heat.
Add chopped onions and minced garlic, sautéing until softened.
Add the callaloo or spinach and cook until wilted.

Stir in the cooked and shredded crab meat. Season with thyme, salt, black pepper, and Scotch bonnet pepper if using. Cook for a few more minutes.
Finish with lime or lemon juice for a burst of freshness. Remove the mixture from heat and let it cool.

Assemble Dumplings:

Divide the rested dough into small balls, approximately the size of a golf ball.
Roll each ball into a small circle, ensuring the edges are thinner than the center.
Place a spoonful of the crab and callaloo mixture in the center of each dough circle.
Fold the dough over the filling to create a half-moon shape and seal the edges by pressing them together. You can crimp the edges for a decorative touch.

Cook Dumplings:

Bring a pot of water to a boil.
Carefully drop the dumplings into the boiling water. Cook until they float to the surface, indicating they are done.
Remove the dumplings with a slotted spoon and let them drain briefly.

Serve:

Serve the Crab and Callaloo Dumplings hot, either on their own or with a dipping sauce of your choice.

These dumplings are a flavorful and satisfying dish, combining the richness of crab meat with the earthy taste of callaloo. They make for a delightful appetizer or main course in Caribbean cuisine.

Souse

Ingredients:

- 2-3 pounds pork trotters, ears, or snout (cleaned and cut into serving-sized pieces)
- 1 cup lime or lemon juice
- 1 cup water
- 2 cucumbers, peeled and sliced
- 1 large red onion, thinly sliced
- 2-3 Scotch bonnet peppers, thinly sliced (adjust to taste)
- 3-4 cloves garlic, minced
- 1 tablespoon fresh thyme leaves
- Salt and black pepper to taste
- 1 cup vinegar (white or apple cider vinegar)
- 1 cup water (for boiling)
- Ice cubes (for serving)

Instructions:

Prepare the Meat:

Rinse the pork trotters, ears, or snout thoroughly under cold water. Cut them into serving-sized pieces.
In a large pot, bring water to a boil. Add the pork pieces and boil for about 10-15 minutes. This helps to remove excess fat and impurities.
Drain the boiled pork and rinse it again under cold water.

Marinate the Meat:

Place the boiled pork pieces in a large bowl.
Pour lime or lemon juice over the pork, ensuring it's well-coated. Let it marinate for about 10-15 minutes.

Prepare the Marinade:

In a separate bowl, combine vinegar, water, sliced cucumbers, sliced red onions, sliced Scotch bonnet peppers, minced garlic, thyme leaves, salt, and black pepper. Mix well.

Pour the marinade over the marinated pork, ensuring all the pieces are submerged. Cover the bowl and let it marinate in the refrigerator for at least 4-6 hours or overnight. The longer it marinates, the more flavorful the souse will be.

Serve:

When ready to serve, remove the souse from the refrigerator and let it come to room temperature.
Serve the souse in bowls, including some of the marinade.
Optionally, add ice cubes to each serving for a refreshing touch.
Souse is often enjoyed with bread or crackers.

Notes:

- Adjust Spice Level: The heat in souse comes from Scotch bonnet peppers. Adjust the quantity according to your spice preference.
- Variations: Some versions of souse may include additional ingredients such as pickled cucumbers, carrots, or green peppers.

Caribbean Souse is a flavorful and zesty dish, perfect for warm weather or as a refreshing appetizer. It's a popular choice for gatherings and celebrations in the Caribbean region.

Peppered Shrimp

Ingredients:

- 1 pound large shrimp, peeled and deveined
- 2 tablespoons vegetable oil
- 4 cloves garlic, minced
- 1-2 Scotch bonnet peppers, finely chopped (adjust to taste)
- 1 teaspoon fresh thyme leaves
- 1 teaspoon paprika
- 1 teaspoon ground cayenne pepper (adjust to spice preference)
- 1 teaspoon ground black pepper
- Salt to taste
- 2 tablespoons chopped fresh parsley or cilantro
- 1 tablespoon lemon or lime juice
- 2 tablespoons unsalted butter

Instructions:

Prepare Shrimp:
- Ensure the shrimp are cleaned, peeled, and deveined. Pat them dry with paper towels.

Season Shrimp:
- In a bowl, combine the minced garlic, chopped Scotch bonnet peppers, fresh thyme leaves, paprika, cayenne pepper, black pepper, and salt. Mix well to create a spice blend.

Marinate Shrimp:
- Toss the shrimp in the spice blend, ensuring they are evenly coated. Allow the shrimp to marinate for at least 15-30 minutes to absorb the flavors.

Cook Shrimp:
- Heat vegetable oil in a large skillet or pan over medium-high heat.
- Add the marinated shrimp to the hot pan, spreading them out in a single layer. Cook for 1-2 minutes on each side until they turn pink and opaque. Be careful not to overcook the shrimp, as they can become tough.

Add Finishing Touches:
- Once the shrimp are cooked, add chopped fresh parsley or cilantro, lemon or lime juice, and unsalted butter to the pan. Toss the shrimp to coat them in the flavorful mixture.

Serve:

- Transfer the Peppered Shrimp to a serving platter and drizzle any remaining sauce over the top.

Garnish (Optional):
- Garnish with additional fresh herbs or a wedge of lemon/lime if desired.

Serve Hot:
- Serve the Peppered Shrimp hot as an appetizer or main course. It pairs well with rice, bread, or a side salad.

Tips:

- Adjust the amount of Scotch bonnet peppers and cayenne pepper to control the level of spiciness.
- Serve the Peppered Shrimp with a cooling dip, such as a garlic aioli or a yogurt-based sauce, to balance the heat.

This Peppered Shrimp recipe captures the bold and fiery flavors of Caribbean cuisine, making it a delicious and memorable dish for seafood enthusiasts.

Banana Fritters

Ingredients:

- 3 ripe bananas
- 1 cup all-purpose flour
- 1 tablespoon sugar
- 1 teaspoon baking powder
- 1/4 teaspoon salt
- 1/2 teaspoon ground cinnamon (optional)
- 1/4 cup milk
- 1 teaspoon vanilla extract
- Vegetable oil for frying
- Powdered sugar for dusting (optional)

Instructions:

Prepare the Bananas:
- Peel the ripe bananas and mash them in a bowl using a fork or potato masher. The bananas should be well-mashed with minimal lumps.

Combine Dry Ingredients:
- In a separate bowl, whisk together the all-purpose flour, sugar, baking powder, salt, and ground cinnamon if using.

Mix Wet Ingredients:
- Add the mashed bananas to the dry ingredients. Pour in the milk and vanilla extract. Mix well until a smooth batter is formed. The batter should have a thick consistency.

Heat Oil:
- In a deep skillet or frying pan, heat enough vegetable oil over medium heat for frying. The oil should be hot but not smoking.

Fry the Banana Fritters:
- Using a spoon or your hands, carefully drop spoonfuls of the banana batter into the hot oil. Flatten them slightly with the back of the spoon.
- Fry the fritters for 2-3 minutes on each side or until they are golden brown and crispy. Ensure they cook evenly by flipping them halfway through the frying process.

Drain Excess Oil:
- Use a slotted spoon to remove the banana fritters from the oil and place them on a plate lined with paper towels to drain any excess oil.

Dust with Powdered Sugar (Optional):

- If desired, dust the banana fritters with powdered sugar while they are still warm.

Serve Warm:
- Banana fritters are best served warm. Enjoy them as a snack or dessert.

Tips:

- Use ripe bananas with brown spots for a sweeter flavor.
- Experiment with additional flavorings such as nutmeg or cardamom for extra depth.

Banana fritters are a delicious way to use up ripe bananas and make for a quick and satisfying treat. They are perfect for breakfast, dessert, or as a sweet snack.

Fish Escabeche

Ingredients:

For the Fried Fish:

- 2 pounds whole fish (such as snapper or grouper), cleaned and scaled
- Salt and pepper to taste
- 1 cup all-purpose flour (for coating)
- Vegetable oil for frying

For the Escabeche Sauce:

- 1 cup white or rice vinegar
- 1/2 cup water
- 1/4 cup sugar
- 1 onion, thinly sliced
- 3 cloves garlic, minced
- 1 red bell pepper, thinly sliced
- 1 carrot, julienned
- 1 bay leaf
- 1 teaspoon whole black peppercorns
- 1 teaspoon salt
- 1/2 teaspoon dried oregano
- 1/2 teaspoon red pepper flakes (optional for heat)

Instructions:

Prepare the Fried Fish:

Clean and scale the whole fish. If using fillets, ensure they are boneless.
Season the fish with salt and pepper.
Coat the fish in flour, shaking off any excess.
In a deep skillet or frying pan, heat enough vegetable oil over medium-high heat for frying.
Fry the fish until golden brown and crispy on both sides. Drain on paper towels to remove excess oil.

Prepare the Escabeche Sauce:

In a saucepan, combine vinegar, water, sugar, onion, garlic, red bell pepper, carrot, bay leaf, whole black peppercorns, salt, oregano, and red pepper flakes if using. Bring the mixture to a boil and then reduce the heat. Simmer for about 5-7 minutes, allowing the vegetables to soften and the flavors to meld.

Remove the saucepan from heat and let the escabeche sauce cool to room temperature.

Once the fried fish and escabeche sauce are both ready and cooled, place the fish in a serving dish and pour the escabeche sauce over it.

Allow the fish to marinate in the sauce for at least 30 minutes to 1 hour before serving. This step helps the flavors to infuse.

Serve:

- Fish Escabeche is typically served at room temperature or slightly chilled.
- Garnish with additional fresh herbs or sliced vegetables if desired.

Notes:

- You can use a mix of vegetables according to your preference.
- Adjust the sweetness, acidity, and spiciness of the escabeche sauce to suit your taste.

Fish Escabeche is a vibrant and flavorful dish that offers a balance of textures and tastes. It's often enjoyed as a main course or appetizer in various cultures.

Pumpkin Soup

Ingredients:

- 2 tablespoons olive oil or butter
- 1 onion, diced
- 2 cloves garlic, minced
- 1 medium-sized pumpkin, peeled, seeded, and diced (about 4 cups)
- 2 carrots, peeled and chopped
- 2 potatoes, peeled and diced
- 4 cups vegetable or chicken broth
- 1 teaspoon ground cumin
- 1/2 teaspoon ground coriander
- 1/2 teaspoon ground nutmeg
- Salt and black pepper to taste
- 1 cup coconut milk (optional, for creaminess)
- Fresh cilantro or parsley for garnish
- Toasted pumpkin seeds for garnish (optional)

Instructions:

Prepare the Vegetables:
- In a large soup pot, heat the olive oil or butter over medium heat. Add the diced onion and garlic, and sauté until softened.

Add Pumpkin and Vegetables:
- Add the diced pumpkin, carrots, and potatoes to the pot. Stir to combine with the onions and garlic.

Season the Vegetables:
- Sprinkle ground cumin, ground coriander, ground nutmeg, salt, and black pepper over the vegetables. Stir to coat the vegetables with the spices.

Pour in Broth:
- Pour the vegetable or chicken broth into the pot. Bring the mixture to a boil, then reduce the heat to simmer. Cover the pot and let it simmer for about 20-25 minutes or until the vegetables are tender.

Blend the Soup:
- Use an immersion blender to puree the soup until smooth. If you don't have an immersion blender, you can carefully transfer the soup to a blender in batches, blending until smooth.

Add Coconut Milk (Optional):

- Stir in the coconut milk if you desire a creamy texture. Adjust the consistency by adding more broth if needed.

Adjust Seasoning:
- Taste the soup and adjust the seasoning, adding more salt and pepper if necessary.

Serve:
- Ladle the pumpkin soup into bowls. Garnish with fresh cilantro or parsley and toasted pumpkin seeds if desired.

Variations:

- Spices: Experiment with other spices like ginger, cinnamon, or curry powder for different flavor profiles.
- Toppings: Serve with a dollop of sour cream, a swirl of yogurt, or a sprinkle of grated cheese.

Pumpkin soup is a versatile dish that can be customized to suit your taste preferences.

It's perfect for warming up on a chilly day and makes for a comforting meal.

Aloo Pie

Ingredients:

For the Dough:

- 2 cups all-purpose flour
- 1/2 teaspoon salt
- 1/4 cup vegetable oil
- Water (enough to make a soft dough)

For the Filling:

- 4 large potatoes, peeled and cubed
- 1 tablespoon vegetable oil
- 1 onion, finely chopped
- 2 cloves garlic, minced
- 1 teaspoon ground cumin
- 1 teaspoon ground coriander
- 1/2 teaspoon turmeric powder
- 1/2 teaspoon garam masala
- Salt and black pepper to taste
- Hot pepper (optional, for heat)
- Chopped cilantro or parsley for garnish

For Frying:

- Vegetable oil for deep frying

Instructions:

Prepare the Dough:

In a bowl, combine the all-purpose flour and salt.
Gradually add vegetable oil and mix until the mixture resembles coarse crumbs.
Add water a little at a time, kneading until you achieve a soft and smooth dough.
Cover the dough and let it rest while you prepare the filling.

Prepare the Filling:

Boil the peeled and cubed potatoes until they are fork-tender. Drain and set aside.

In a pan, heat vegetable oil over medium heat. Add chopped onions and sauté until softened.

Add minced garlic and sauté for an additional minute.

Stir in ground cumin, ground coriander, turmeric powder, garam masala, salt, black pepper, and hot pepper if using.

Add the boiled potatoes to the spice mixture, mashing them and combining everything well. Cook for a few minutes until the flavors meld.

Remove the filling from heat and let it cool.

Assemble and Fry:

Divide the dough into small balls, about the size of a golf ball.

Roll out each ball into a small circle.

Place a spoonful of the potato filling in the center of each dough circle.

Fold the dough over the filling, creating a semi-circle shape. Seal the edges by pressing them together.

Heat vegetable oil in a deep pot or frying pan for deep frying.

Carefully drop the filled dough into the hot oil and fry until golden brown on both sides.

Remove the Aloo Pie from the oil using a slotted spoon and place them on a plate lined with paper towels to drain any excess oil.

Garnish with chopped cilantro or parsley.

Serve:

Serve Aloo Pie hot on its own or with your favorite chutney or dipping sauce.

Aloo Pie is a delicious and satisfying snack with a perfect blend of spices. It's a popular street food item in Trinidad and Tobago, often enjoyed by locals and visitors alike.

Grilled Lobster

Ingredients:

- 2 whole lobsters (about 1 to 1.5 pounds each)
- 1/2 cup unsalted butter, melted
- 2 cloves garlic, minced
- 1 tablespoon fresh lemon juice
- Salt and black pepper to taste
- Fresh parsley, chopped (for garnish)
- Lemon wedges (for serving)

Instructions:

Prepare the Lobsters:
- If your lobsters are still alive, you'll need to humanely dispatch them before cooking. You can do this by placing them in the freezer for about 30 minutes before cooking.

Split the Lobsters:
- Using a sharp knife or kitchen shears, split the lobsters in half lengthwise. Remove the vein-like digestive tract if visible.

Prepare the Butter Sauce:
- In a small bowl, mix melted butter, minced garlic, and fresh lemon juice. Season with salt and black pepper to taste.

Preheat the Grill:
- Preheat your grill to medium-high heat. Make sure the grates are clean and well-oiled to prevent sticking.

Brush with Butter Sauce:
- Brush the lobster halves with the prepared butter sauce, ensuring they are well-coated.

Grill the Lobster:
- Place the lobster halves on the preheated grill, cut side down. Grill for about 4-5 minutes until the edges begin to char.
- Flip the lobster halves and brush the exposed flesh with more butter sauce. Grill for an additional 4-5 minutes or until the lobster meat is opaque and cooked through.

Garnish and Serve:
- Remove the grilled lobster halves from the grill and place them on a serving platter.

- Drizzle any remaining butter sauce over the lobster and garnish with chopped fresh parsley.

Serve with Lemon Wedges:
- Serve the grilled lobster immediately with lemon wedges on the side for squeezing over the lobster meat.

Tips:

- Grill Temperature: Cooking times may vary depending on your grill's temperature. Adjust accordingly to achieve a perfect char without overcooking the lobster.
- Flavor Variations: Experiment with different herb-infused butter sauces or add a pinch of cayenne pepper for a spicy kick.

Grilled lobster is an elegant and indulgent dish that's perfect for special occasions or a delightful seafood feast. Enjoy the rich and flavorful lobster meat enhanced by the smokiness of the grill.

Pineapple Upside-Down Cake

Ingredients:

For the Pineapple Topping:

- 1/2 cup unsalted butter
- 1 cup brown sugar, packed
- 1 can (20 oz) pineapple slices in juice, drained (reserve the juice)
- Maraschino cherries (optional, for decoration)

For the Cake Batter:

- 1 and 1/2 cups all-purpose flour
- 1 and 1/2 teaspoons baking powder
- 1/2 teaspoon baking soda
- 1/4 teaspoon salt
- 1/2 cup unsalted butter, softened
- 1 cup granulated sugar
- 2 large eggs
- 1 teaspoon vanilla extract
- 1/2 cup sour cream
- 1/2 cup pineapple juice (from the drained can)

Instructions:

Preheat the Oven:

Preheat your oven to 350°F (175°C).

Prepare the Pineapple Topping:

In a saucepan, melt 1/2 cup of unsalted butter over medium heat.
Add the brown sugar to the melted butter, stirring until well combined and slightly caramelized. Remove from heat.
Pour the caramelized mixture into the bottom of a greased 9-inch round cake pan, spreading it evenly.
Arrange pineapple slices on top of the caramel, placing a maraschino cherry in the center of each pineapple ring if desired.

Prepare the Cake Batter:

In a medium bowl, whisk together the all-purpose flour, baking powder, baking soda, and salt. Set aside.

In a large bowl, cream together 1/2 cup softened butter and granulated sugar until light and fluffy.

Add the eggs one at a time, beating well after each addition. Stir in the vanilla extract.

Gradually add the dry ingredients to the wet ingredients, alternating with the sour cream and pineapple juice. Begin and end with the dry ingredients, mixing until just combined.

Assemble and Bake:

Pour the batter over the pineapple slices in the cake pan, spreading it evenly.

Bake in the preheated oven for 40-45 minutes or until a toothpick inserted into the center comes out clean.

Allow the cake to cool in the pan for 10-15 minutes.

Invert the cake onto a serving platter, carefully removing the pan.

Let the Pineapple Upside-Down Cake cool completely before slicing and serving.

Tips:

- Ensure the butter and sugar for the topping are melted and well combined to create a smooth caramel.
- Use a toothpick or cake tester to check for doneness by inserting it into the center of the cake. It should come out clean when the cake is fully baked.

Pineapple Upside-Down Cake is a timeless dessert that's both visually appealing and delicious. Enjoy the sweet and tangy pineapple flavors combined with the moist cake for a delightful treat.

Seafood Roti

Ingredients:

For the Roti:

- 3 cups all-purpose flour
- 1 teaspoon baking powder
- 1 teaspoon salt
- Water (enough to make a soft dough)
- Vegetable oil (for cooking)

For the Seafood Filling:

- 1 pound mixed seafood (shrimp, fish, squid, etc.), cleaned and cut into bite-sized pieces
- 1 onion, finely chopped
- 2 cloves garlic, minced
- 1 bell pepper, diced
- 1 tomato, diced
- 1 cup coconut milk
- 1 tablespoon curry powder
- 1 teaspoon ground cumin
- 1 teaspoon ground coriander
- 1 teaspoon turmeric
- Salt and black pepper to taste
- 2 tablespoons vegetable oil

Optional Garnishes:

- Chopped fresh cilantro or parsley
- Hot pepper sauce

Instructions:

Prepare the Roti Dough:

In a large bowl, combine the all-purpose flour, baking powder, and salt.

Gradually add water, mixing continuously until a soft and pliable dough is formed.
Knead the dough for a few minutes until it becomes smooth.
Divide the dough into golf ball-sized portions. Roll each portion into a smooth ball.
Roll out each ball into a thin, flat disc (roti) using a rolling pin.
Heat a griddle or non-stick pan over medium-high heat. Cook each roti for about 1-2 minutes on each side or until they puff up and develop a few brown spots.
Brush each roti with a bit of vegetable oil during cooking.

Prepare the Seafood Filling:

In a large skillet, heat vegetable oil over medium heat.
Add chopped onions and minced garlic, sautéing until softened.
Add the mixed seafood to the skillet and cook until they start to turn opaque.
Stir in diced bell pepper and tomato, cooking for an additional 2-3 minutes.
Sprinkle curry powder, ground cumin, ground coriander, turmeric, salt, and black pepper over the seafood mixture. Mix well to coat the seafood evenly.
Pour in the coconut milk and let the mixture simmer for about 5-7 minutes or until the seafood is fully cooked and the flavors meld.

Assemble the Seafood Roti:

Place a portion of the seafood filling in the center of each roti.
Fold the sides of the roti over the filling, creating a square or rectangular shape.
Serve the Seafood Roti hot, garnished with chopped cilantro or parsley and accompanied by hot pepper sauce if desired.

Tips:

- Customize the seafood filling by using your favorite combination of seafood.
- Adjust the level of spiciness by adding more or less hot pepper to the filling.

Seafood Roti is a delicious and satisfying dish that brings together the rich flavors of seafood with the soft and flaky texture of the roti. It's a fantastic option for those who enjoy Caribbean cuisine.

www.ingramcontent.com/pod-product-compliance
Lightning Source LLC
LaVergne TN
LVHW081608060526
838201LV00054B/2140